# Life in Multinational Companies

C. P. Kumar
Reiki Healer
Roorkee - 247667, India

# Disclaimer

While every effort has been made to ensure the accuracy and completeness of the content in this book, the author cannot guarantee that the information contained herein is error-free, up-to-date, or suitable for every individual circumstance.

The author shall not be held liable or responsible for any errors or omissions in the content of the book, nor for any damages, or losses that may arise from any actions taken based upon the suggestions or contents presented in the book.

Readers are advised to use their own judgment and discretion in applying the information provided in this book, and to consult with qualified professionals before taking any action based on the contents of this book. The author disclaims any and all liability or responsibility for any actions taken or not taken based on the information contained in this book.

# DEDICATION

To the dedicated and resilient individuals who navigate the complex and ever-evolving landscape of multinational companies, this book is lovingly dedicated to you. Your unwavering commitment to bridging cultural divides, fostering diversity and inclusivity, and adapting to the challenges and opportunities that come with global employment is truly inspiring.

In your pursuit of excellence, you have embarked on a journey that transcends borders, connecting people from all corners of the world. Your experiences and insights are the heart and soul of this book, which aims to shed light on the multifaceted aspects of life in multinational companies.

Your commitment to understanding the intricacies of cross-cultural communication, promoting gender equality and diversity, nurturing talent, and supporting mental well-being is vital to the success of multinational corporations. As this book explores the diverse topics within your professional world, we hope to honor your dedication and provide valuable knowledge to support your endeavors.

Your resilience in the face of change, your pursuit of a balanced work-life harmony, and your role in shaping the future of work exemplify the spirit of global collaboration and innovation. With profound gratitude and admiration for your contributions, we dedicate this book to the remarkable individuals who make multinational companies not just places of work, but vibrant hubs of cultural exchange and growth.

May the insights shared within these pages empower you, inspire you, and help you thrive in your unique professional journey within the dynamic world of multinational companies. Your commitment to global success is a testament to your unwavering dedication, and this book is a small tribute to your incredible efforts.

**C. P. Kumar**

# CONTENTS

# PREFACE

In a world characterized by interconnectivity and globalization, multinational companies (MNCs) stand as prominent pillars of our global economy. These entities bring together an array of cultures and backgrounds, creating a mosaic of diversity within their workforce. "Life in Multinational Companies" offers an extensive exploration of this intricate world, guiding you through the dynamic interplay of cultures, global mobility, inclusivity, and the ever-evolving nature of work within these colossal organizations.

The overarching purpose of this book is to provide readers with a comprehensive and insightful perspective of life within MNCs. It acts as a guiding compass, illuminating the labyrinthine corridors of corporate dynamics. While refraining from specific details about individual chapters, we aim to offer an overview of the book's significance and relevance.

The significance of this book lies in its role as a gateway to understanding the unique and complex ecosystem of MNCs. It presents a holistic view of the challenges and opportunities that arise in the wake of globalization, and how MNCs adapt to these circumstances.

Our journey begins with an introduction to MNCs and the rich diversity that characterizes their workforces. We then delve into the intricate aspects of cultural diversity, inclusivity, global mobility, and the pivotal role of expatriates in these organizations. As we traverse through these topics, we gain a deep understanding of how MNCs function and how they create environments that foster inclusivity and innovation.

The subsequent chapters explore human resources practices, work-life balance, career development, compensation, gender equality, mentorship, cross-cultural communication, employee well-being, performance evaluation, employee engagement, and conflict resolution within MNCs. Each chapter contributes to our understanding of the multifaceted dimensions of life within these organizations.

Furthermore, our exploration extends to the future of work, where we uncover emerging trends and challenges within MNCs. This final chapter acts as a beacon, shedding light on the ever-evolving landscape of global business.

Ultimately, this book serves as a valuable resource for individuals aspiring to work in MNCs, professionals already navigating this intricate terrain, and anyone interested in understanding the global business environment. "Life in Multinational Companies" offers readers the opportunity to explore the vibrant mosaic of cultures, strategies, and challenges that define life within these influential organizations. It is our hope that, by embarking on this journey, you will gain a deeper appreciation for the global workforce and the significance of MNCs in shaping our interconnected world.

**C. P. Kumar**
Reiki Healer
Former Scientist 'G', National Institute of Hydrology
Roorkee - 247667, India
Web: https://www.angelfire.com/nh/cpkumar/virgo.html

# Chapter 1. Introduction to Multinational Companies and Their Workforces

Multinational companies (MNCs) have become a fundamental aspect of the modern global economy, playing a pivotal role in shaping international business, trade, and employment practices. Their operations transcend national boundaries, reaching across various countries, cultures, and regions. This article delves into the intriguing world of multinational companies and the diverse workforces that power their success.

## Defining Multinational Companies

Multinational companies, often abbreviated as MNCs or referred to as multinational corporations (MNCs), are large corporations that operate in multiple countries simultaneously. These companies are not bound by the constraints of a single national market but have established a global presence through subsidiaries, affiliates, or branches in various nations. MNCs differ from purely domestic companies, which focus primarily on one national market, by their ability to navigate the complexities of international business.

MNCs often serve as key drivers of globalization, a phenomenon that has been accelerating over the past few decades. These companies leverage their financial and operational resources to expand beyond their home country, aiming to capture a share of international markets. They engage in various sectors, from technology and manufacturing to finance and healthcare, and they often hold a prominent position in the global economy.

**The Diversity of Global Workforces**

One of the most distinctive characteristics of multinational companies is their ability to build and manage diverse global workforces. The employees of MNCs can be drawn from various nationalities and cultural backgrounds, reflecting the wide array of locations in which these corporations operate. This diversity brings both challenges and opportunities to MNCs and their employees.

1. Cultural Diversity

MNCs employ individuals from different parts of the world, each bringing their unique cultural perspectives, traditions, and values to the workplace. This rich cultural tapestry can lead to a dynamic work environment, but it also necessitates the development of intercultural competencies among employees and management. Cultural diversity can bring innovation and creativity to the workplace, fostering a broader range of perspectives and problem-solving approaches.

However, it can also present challenges, including communication barriers, misunderstandings, and the potential for cultural clashes. MNCs must invest in training programs and cultural sensitivity initiatives to ensure that their diverse workforce functions cohesively and harmoniously.

2. Language Diversity

Language is a fundamental aspect of communication, and in MNCs, it can be a significant factor in the workplace. Employees may need to communicate with colleagues, clients, and partners from different linguistic backgrounds.

As a result, language diversity can be both an asset and a challenge for MNCs.

Multinational companies often require employees to be proficient in a common business language, such as English. However, fluency in multiple languages is an advantage, particularly in regions where different languages are commonly spoken. MNCs may also use translation services and technologies to bridge language gaps in the workplace.

## 3. Legal and Regulatory Diversity

Operating in multiple countries means navigating an intricate web of legal and regulatory systems. Each nation has its own set of rules and regulations governing employment, taxation, intellectual property, and more. This legal diversity poses a complex challenge for MNCs, necessitating the need for legal departments or consultants well-versed in international law.

Furthermore, MNCs must stay abreast of changes in laws and regulations in each country where they operate to ensure compliance. Non-compliance can result in financial penalties, damage to the company's reputation, and even expulsion from certain markets.

## 4. Economic Diversity

The economic diversity among the countries where MNCs operate can be vast. Some countries may have well-developed economies with a stable financial system, while others may be emerging markets with higher levels of economic volatility. Multinational companies must adapt their strategies to suit the economic conditions of each country they engage with.

This includes pricing strategies, currency risk management, and the ability to allocate resources effectively to optimize profitability. Economic diversity also means that MNCs can benefit from varied opportunities for growth and expansion in different markets.

## 5. Workforce Mobility

Workforce mobility is a hallmark of multinational companies. Employees often have the opportunity to travel or be relocated to different locations as part of their career growth or specific project requirements. This mobility can be an attractive aspect of working for an MNC, offering individuals the chance to experience new cultures, broaden their skills, and expand their global network.

However, it also brings challenges, particularly related to family considerations, work-life balance, and adaptation to new environments. MNCs must support employees who relocate, offering assistance with housing, schooling for children, and cultural integration to ensure the transition is as smooth as possible.

## 6. Benefits and Compensation

The benefits and compensation packages offered by MNCs often differ from those of purely domestic companies. To attract and retain top talent, MNCs typically offer competitive international compensation packages, which may include benefits like housing allowances, relocation assistance, and educational support for expatriate employees. This compensation structure is designed to make international assignments attractive to employees and to provide them with the resources they need to adapt to a new country.

Multinational companies also face unique ethical and social responsibility challenges. Their global operations can be subject to scrutiny from a variety of stakeholders, including governments, non-governmental organizations (NGOs), and the public. Issues related to labor practices, environmental impact, and human rights can have far-reaching consequences on a company's reputation and financial performance.

MNCs must prioritize ethical and sustainable business practices and consider the societal and environmental impact of their operations. Many multinational companies have established corporate social responsibility (CSR) initiatives to demonstrate their commitment to making a positive impact in the communities where they operate.

**Conclusion**

Multinational companies are a fascinating and integral part of the modern global business landscape. Their ability to operate across borders and manage diverse global workforces reflects the interconnectedness of the world's economies and societies. The diversity present in MNCs, whether it be cultural, linguistic, legal, or economic, presents both challenges and opportunities for these organizations.

MNCs must continuously adapt to changing global conditions, while ensuring they remain compliant with diverse legal and regulatory systems. In doing so, they can leverage the benefits of global expansion and economic diversity to achieve long-term success. Furthermore, by embracing cultural and language diversity and implementing ethical and socially responsible practices, multinational companies can foster innovation and goodwill, contributing to the well-being of the communities they touch.

As the world continues to evolve, multinational companies will play a vital role in shaping the future of international business, economies, and societies. Their workforces, drawn from the far corners of the globe, are a testament to the power of diversity and collaboration on a global scale. Understanding the intricacies of MNCs and their workforces is essential for those looking to engage with or work within this dynamic and influential sector of the global economy.

# Chapter 2. Cultural Diversity and Inclusivity in Multinational Companies

## Introduction

Multinational companies (MNCs) have become synonymous with the global business landscape. These organizations operate across borders, transcending geographical and cultural boundaries. However, this globalization brings with it an unparalleled level of diversity, both in terms of their market reach and their internal workforce. Embracing cultural diversity and fostering inclusivity has become paramount for these entities. This article explores the profound impact of diverse workforces on company culture, the strategies MNCs employ to promote inclusivity, and the lasting benefits these practices can bring.

## The Impact of Diverse Workforces on Company Culture

Diversity in the workplace has evolved from being just a buzzword to an essential element of modern organizations. Multinational companies, by their very nature, tend to be more diverse than smaller enterprises. Their employees often hail from different countries, ethnic backgrounds, and cultural contexts. This diversity, when harnessed effectively, can significantly influence company culture.

### 1. Enhanced Creativity and Innovation

Diverse teams bring together individuals with varying perspectives and experiences. This diversity of thought can lead to the generation of innovative ideas and solutions.

When employees from different backgrounds collaborate, they are more likely to think outside the box and offer fresh, creative approaches to challenges.

## 2. Improved Decision-Making

Diverse workforces can make better decisions. They tend to consider a broader range of factors and viewpoints when making choices. This can lead to more comprehensive, balanced, and ultimately, effective decisions. It prevents groupthink and encourages critical evaluation.

## 3. Increased Market Adaptability

For multinational companies, adapting to new markets is essential. A diverse workforce can offer valuable insights into local customs, preferences, and business practices. This knowledge is critical for tailoring products and services to specific markets, ultimately increasing the company's competitiveness.

## 4. Customer Understanding

A multicultural workforce is more likely to understand the cultural nuances of a diverse customer base. This understanding can lead to better customer relations, as employees can communicate and empathize effectively with clients from different backgrounds.

## 5. Improved Employee Satisfaction

Inclusive workplaces that embrace diversity often have higher levels of employee satisfaction. When individuals feel accepted and valued for who they are, it fosters a positive work environment. This, in turn, leads to increased morale and productivity.

## 6. Talent Attraction and Retention

Companies that prioritize diversity and inclusivity tend to attract a wider pool of talent. Potential employees are more likely to be drawn to organizations where they see people like themselves succeeding. Moreover, once hired, diverse employees are more likely to stay with companies that value their unique perspectives and contributions.

**Strategies for Fostering Inclusivity**

To harness the potential benefits of diversity, multinational companies must implement strategies that foster inclusivity. Here are some effective approaches:

## 1. Diversity Training

MNCs can provide diversity and inclusion training to all employees. These programs educate individuals about the importance of diversity, the benefits it brings, and how to work effectively in a diverse environment. They can also address unconscious bias, promoting self-awareness among employees.

## 2. Inclusive Leadership

Leadership plays a crucial role in creating an inclusive culture. Executives and managers should lead by example, actively promoting diversity and inclusivity. They can set the tone by actively engaging with employees from various backgrounds, listening to their concerns, and ensuring their voices are heard.

## 3. Employee Resource Groups (ERGs)

Many MNCs create ERGs, which are voluntary, employee-led groups that focus on supporting and promoting diversity and inclusivity within the company. ERGs can provide a sense of belonging for employees and offer valuable insights to the organization.

## 4. Equal Opportunities

It's essential to ensure that everyone has equal opportunities for career advancement and development. This means creating a level playing field for all employees, regardless of their background. Promotion and hiring decisions should be based on merit, skills, and experience rather than biases.

## 5. Flexible Work Arrangements

Recognizing that employees have diverse needs, multinational companies can provide flexible work arrangements to accommodate individual circumstances. This approach supports a diverse workforce, which includes people with different lifestyles, family commitments, and personal preferences.

## 6. Transparent Communication

Open and transparent communication is essential in promoting inclusivity. Employees should feel comfortable discussing their concerns, sharing ideas, and reporting any instances of discrimination or bias. Multinational companies should have clear channels for these discussions.

7. Supplier and Partner Inclusivity

Inclusivity extends beyond the company's internal operations. Multinational companies can also foster diversity among their suppliers and partners. By choosing diverse suppliers and collaborators, they support the broader ecosystem of inclusivity.

8. Mentorship and Sponsorship Programs

MNCs can establish mentorship and sponsorship programs to support the career growth of underrepresented employees. These programs provide guidance, networking opportunities, and advocacy, helping diverse individuals advance in their careers.

**Conclusion**

Cultural diversity and inclusivity are not mere corporate buzzwords for multinational companies. They are essential components that can have a profound impact on the company's culture, performance, and long-term success. Embracing diversity not only enhances creativity and innovation but also improves decision-making and market adaptability. Additionally, it fosters better employee satisfaction and can help attract and retain top talent.

To harness these benefits, MNCs must adopt various strategies. Diversity training, inclusive leadership, employee resource groups, and equal opportunities are just a few of the many approaches they can take. The ultimate goal is to create an environment where every employee feels valued, respected, and empowered to contribute their unique perspectives to the company's success.

In today's globalized world, multinational companies that prioritize cultural diversity and inclusivity are better equipped to navigate the challenges and opportunities of the international marketplace. They not only adapt to diverse markets more effectively but also establish themselves as leaders in promoting social progress and equality in the corporate world. As MNCs continue to expand their global footprint, their commitment to diversity and inclusivity will become an even more critical factor in their long-term success and impact on society.

# Chapter 3. Global Mobility and Expatriate Assignments

## Introduction

Multinational companies (MNCs) have become a cornerstone of the modern global economy. These corporate giants transcend national borders, and their operations span across various countries. One crucial element that fuels the international expansion of MNCs is the strategic use of expatriate assignments. Expatriates, often called "global mobility talent", play an integral role in bridging the gap between headquarters and overseas subsidiaries, facilitating the transfer of knowledge and best practices, and ensuring effective global operations. This article delves into the role of expatriates in MNCs, explores the challenges and benefits of global mobility, and concludes by emphasizing the pivotal role they play in shaping the world of multinational business.

## The Role of Expatriates in MNCs

Expatriates are employees of a multinational company who are assigned to work in foreign countries for a specific period, ranging from a few months to several years. Their primary role is to facilitate the international expansion and global operations of the company. The multifaceted role of expatriates in MNCs can be summarized as follows:

Knowledge Transfer and Skill Development: Expatriates serve as a conduit for the transfer of knowledge, skills, and best practices from the company's headquarters to its overseas subsidiaries. They are responsible for disseminating corporate culture, values, and operational strategies, ensuring that global standards are maintained across all locations.

Cross-Cultural Communication: A vital part of the expatriate's role is fostering cross-cultural communication within the organization. They help bridge cultural gaps between the headquarters and local employees in foreign subsidiaries, promoting mutual understanding and collaboration.

Talent Development and Leadership: Expatriate assignments are often used as a means of developing future leaders within the organization. The exposure to international experiences and challenges helps employees acquire essential leadership skills and adapt to diverse working environments.

Project Implementation and Control: Expatriates are often entrusted with overseeing critical projects in foreign subsidiaries, ensuring that they align with the company's strategic objectives and are executed in a manner consistent with corporate standards.

Local Talent Management: In addition to their role in knowledge transfer, expatriates are expected to identify and groom local talent, creating a sustainable talent pipeline in the host country.

**Challenges and Benefits of Global Mobility**

While the role of expatriates in MNCs is crucial, it is not without its challenges. Global mobility can be demanding and present numerous hurdles for both the individuals and the organizations. However, these challenges are often accompanied by significant benefits.

## 1. Challenges of Global Mobility

**Cultural Adjustment**: Moving to a foreign country means adapting to a new culture, language, and way of life. Cultural adjustment can be challenging and may result in stress and frustration for expatriates and their families.

**Family Considerations**: Expatriate assignments often entail relocating the entire family, which can be disruptive and stressful for spouses and children. Ensuring the well-being and happiness of family members is a critical concern.

**Isolation**: Expatriates may feel isolated or disconnected from their home country, friends, and social support networks. Loneliness and feelings of isolation can affect job performance and personal well-being.

**Work-Life Balance**: Balancing the demands of an international career with personal life can be challenging. Expatriates may experience long working hours and frequent travel, which can strain family relationships.

**Legal and Administrative Issues**: Dealing with immigration, work permits, and tax-related matters in a foreign country can be complex and time-consuming. Navigating legal and administrative hurdles is a significant challenge.

## 2. Benefits of Global Mobility

**Personal and Professional Growth**: Expatriate assignments provide employees with the opportunity for personal and professional growth. They gain valuable international experience, develop cross-cultural skills, and broaden their horizons.

Career Advancement: An international assignment can fast-track an employee's career within the organization. Those who successfully complete assignments abroad often have a competitive advantage when vying for leadership roles.

Knowledge and Skill Transfer: Expatriates facilitate the transfer of knowledge and skills across borders, ensuring that the company's best practices are maintained consistently in different locations.

Enhanced Global Perspective: Expatriates gain a deeper understanding of global markets, trends, and consumer behaviors, which can inform the company's strategic decision-making.

Improved Cross-Cultural Communication: Working in diverse environments sharpens the expatriate's ability to communicate and collaborate with individuals from different cultural backgrounds, a skill that is highly valuable in a global business context.

**Conclusion**

In today's interconnected world, the role of expatriates in multinational companies is more critical than ever. They act as the linchpin connecting the organization's headquarters with its overseas subsidiaries, facilitating knowledge transfer, promoting cross-cultural communication, and driving the company's global agenda.

However, the challenges that expatriates face should not be underestimated. The personal and professional demands of global mobility are substantial, from adapting to a new culture and ensuring family well-being to navigating legal and administrative issues. It's crucial for MNCs to provide adequate support and resources to help expatriates overcome these challenges.

The benefits of global mobility, on the other hand, are substantial. Expatriates gain valuable personal and professional growth, which ultimately benefits the organization. Their knowledge and skill transfer are invaluable in maintaining consistent standards across borders, and their enhanced global perspective can inform strategic decision-making.

In conclusion, expatriate assignments are a cornerstone of multinational business success. They are the catalysts that drive the global expansion of MNCs, foster cross-cultural collaboration, and ensure that the company's vision is realized on a global scale. While the challenges are real, the benefits far outweigh them, making expatriates indispensable assets in the dynamic world of multinational companies.

# Chapter 4. HR Practices in Multinational Companies

## Introduction

In today's globalized world, multinational companies have become a driving force in the world economy. These organizations operate in diverse cultural landscapes, and managing their workforce efficiently is a critical factor in their success. Human Resource (HR) practices in multinational companies play a pivotal role in achieving and maintaining a competitive edge. In this article, we will explore various aspects of HR practices within these companies, including recruitment and selection of international talent, cross-cultural training and development, and their significance in ensuring the smooth functioning and growth of multinational corporations.

## Recruitment and Selection of International Talent

The recruitment and selection of international talent is a cornerstone of HR practices in multinational companies. A diverse and skilled workforce is essential for global organizations as they operate in different markets with distinct requirements. Let's delve into some key aspects of this critical HR function:

Global Talent Acquisition Strategies: Multinational companies need a well-defined talent acquisition strategy that spans borders. These strategies often involve establishing talent pipelines, both locally and internationally, and leveraging networks, job portals, and partnerships with educational institutions. They aim to attract the best talent from different regions, reflecting the global nature of the business.

Cultural Fit and Diversity: While technical skills and experience are essential, cultural fit is equally important. Multinational companies seek individuals who not only possess the necessary competencies but also align with the organization's core values and culture. Embracing diversity in hiring ensures a richer perspective within the organization and helps adapt to various local market dynamics.

Language Proficiency: Many multinational companies require their employees to be proficient in English, which is often the business lingua franca. However, they also value proficiency in local languages, as this can be a significant asset in understanding and connecting with local markets.

Cross-Border Legal and Compliance Knowledge: HR teams in multinational companies must be well-versed in international employment laws, visa regulations, and work permits. This knowledge is crucial to ensure legal compliance in different countries and to prevent any potential legal complications.

Global Onboarding Processes: Onboarding is the process of integrating and orienting new employees into an organization, ensuring they are familiar with its culture, policies, and their roles and responsibilities. Effective onboarding is critical, as it sets the tone for an employee's journey within the organization. Multinational companies often have standardized onboarding processes that integrate local nuances, which can help international employees feel more comfortable and acclimated to their new environment.

## Cross-Cultural Training and Development

Managing a diverse workforce in multinational companies comes with its own set of challenges. Cultural differences can sometimes lead to misunderstandings or miscommunications, potentially affecting productivity and collaboration. To address these issues, cross-cultural training and development programs are essential. Here's a closer look at this vital aspect of HR practices:

Cultural Sensitivity Training: Many multinational organizations provide cultural sensitivity training to their employees, helping them understand and appreciate different cultures and the nuances of working in diverse environments. This training can include aspects like communication styles, social norms, and business etiquette in different countries.

Language Training: To facilitate smoother communication, multinational companies may offer language training programs for employees, especially when working in regions where English is not the primary language. Language skills are invaluable when it comes to building relationships and understanding local markets.

Global Leadership Development: HR in multinational companies often invests in developing global leaders who can navigate and lead teams across cultures. This includes fostering leadership skills that are adaptable and culturally sensitive. These leaders are instrumental in bridging cultural gaps and driving international teams to success.

Mentorship and Buddy Programs: Mentorship and buddy programs are structured approaches to provide support and guidance to individuals, typically in a workplace or educational setting. In a *mentorship program*, an experienced and knowledgeable person (mentor) guides and advises a less experienced individual (mentee) to help them develop their skills, knowledge, and career. A *buddy program* pairs new or inexperienced individuals with peers or colleagues (buddies) who can offer immediate assistance, answer questions, and provide a friendly, informal support system as they navigate their roles or environment. Establishing mentorship and buddy programs can help international employees integrate more effectively. These programs connect them with local colleagues who can offer guidance and support, both professionally and personally.

Diversity and Inclusion Initiatives: Multinational companies are increasingly embracing diversity and inclusion initiatives to create a harmonious work environment. HR plays a pivotal role in developing policies and programs that promote diversity, equity, and inclusion, ensuring all employees feel valued and respected.

**Conclusion**

In conclusion, HR practices in multinational companies are fundamental to their success in the global marketplace. The recruitment and selection of international talent, as well as cross-cultural training and development, are two key pillars of these practices.

Recruitment strategies must align with the company's global objectives and emphasize the importance of cultural fit and diversity. The ability to navigate international employment laws and work permits is essential, as is providing a standardized yet culturally sensitive onboarding process.

Cross-cultural training and development programs are equally vital in helping employees understand and adapt to the diverse environments they work in. These programs foster cultural sensitivity, language proficiency, and global leadership skills. In addition, mentorship, diversity and inclusion initiatives, and other programs work together to create an inclusive, supportive, and productive work environment.

In today's world, where multinational companies are expanding and competing on a global scale, their HR practices serve as a linchpin for sustained success. A workforce that is not only highly skilled but also culturally attuned is a strategic asset that can help these organizations thrive in diverse and dynamic markets. As multinational companies continue to evolve, their HR practices will remain at the forefront of shaping their future, fostering innovation, and sustaining growth.

## Introduction

In today's rapidly evolving global workforce, achieving work-life balance has become a paramount concern for employees and employers alike. The advent of multinational companies has transformed the way we work, connecting professionals from diverse corners of the world. As organizations expand their operations internationally, employees often find themselves navigating through time zones, cultures, and expectations. This shift has introduced new challenges and opportunities for achieving equilibrium between work commitments and personal life. In this article, we will explore the complexities of work-life balance in a global workforce and delve into strategies, such as flexible work arrangements and remote work, that can facilitate its attainment.

## Balancing Work Demands with Personal and Family Life

One of the primary concerns in multinational corporations is the struggle to balance the ever-increasing demands of work with personal and family life. The global workforce often finds itself confronting unique challenges in this regard.

Cultural Differences: Multinational companies operate in diverse cultural settings, and employees are exposed to varying work cultures and expectations. These cultural differences can create friction when trying to balance work with personal life. For instance, some cultures may emphasize long working hours and prioritize professional commitments over personal time, while others may have a more balanced approach.

To overcome these cultural hurdles, employees need to adapt and adopt a flexible mindset. Understanding and respecting the cultural norms of the organization and the host country can help individuals navigate these differences and establish a work-life balance that aligns with their values.

Time Zone Challenges: Global workforces often involve collaboration across multiple time zones. Coordinating meetings, deadlines, and project handovers can be daunting when your colleagues are located in different parts of the world. This can lead to long and irregular working hours, making it challenging to allocate time for personal and family life.

To address this issue, companies should adopt time zone-sensitive policies and practices. Employers can encourage employees to set specific working hours based on their local time zones, and meetings can be scheduled with consideration for these time differences. This approach helps ensure that employees can be productive during their regular hours and still have time for personal life.

Travel Requirements: Many global positions require extensive travel. While this may seem glamorous to some, it can be disruptive to personal and family life. Frequent travel can lead to exhaustion, strain on personal relationships, and difficulties in maintaining a consistent work-life balance.

To mitigate the impact of travel on work-life balance, companies should develop clear travel policies that take into account employees' needs and preferences. Providing employees with the option to choose their travel frequency and ensuring that they have adequate time for recovery and reconnection with their families is crucial in maintaining equilibrium.

## Flexible Work Arrangements and Remote Work

In the pursuit of work-life balance in a global workforce, flexible work arrangements and remote work have emerged as pivotal strategies.

Flextime and Compressed Workweeks: Flexible work arrangements, such as flextime and compressed workweeks, allow employees to adjust their working hours to better suit their personal and family needs. *Flextime* is a work arrangement that allows employees to adjust their daily start and end times within set limits, offering greater schedule flexibility. *Compressed workweek* is an alternative work schedule condensing the standard 5-day workweek into fewer days, typically involving longer work hours on those days to provide extended time off. These arrangements can be particularly beneficial for parents who need to accommodate school schedules or caregivers who need to tend to family members.

Multinational companies can implement these arrangements by setting core hours for collaboration and allowing employees to adapt their schedules around them. This approach gives employees the autonomy to balance their work and personal commitments effectively.

Telecommuting and Remote Work: The rise of remote work has been one of the most significant shifts in the global workforce, and it offers unique opportunities to achieve work-life balance. Remote work allows employees to work from anywhere, reducing the need for long commutes and providing greater flexibility.

To ensure the success of remote work, companies should invest in robust technology infrastructure and encourage open communication channels. It is essential for remote employees to feel connected to their colleagues and have access to the necessary tools and resources to perform their tasks effectively.

Job Sharing and Part-Time Options: *Job sharing* is a work arrangement where two or more employees share the responsibilities of a single full-time position, allowing for reduced individual work hours and increased work-life balance. *Part-time option* refers to employment that involves working fewer hours than a standard full-time position, enabling individuals to balance work with other commitments or interests. Job sharing and part-time positions are effective solutions for employees who seek to balance their work commitments with family or personal life. These arrangements allow two or more individuals to share responsibilities for a single role, or employees can work part-time while maintaining their position.

Multinational companies can explore job-sharing programs to retain experienced employees who may otherwise leave due to family or personal commitments. Part-time positions can be made available to provide flexibility without compromising productivity.

Global Mobility and Transfer Policies: Multinational companies should also consider their global mobility and transfer policies. When employees are transferred to international locations, there are unique challenges that can affect their work-life balance. Companies need to offer comprehensive support in areas such as housing, education for dependents, and social integration to ensure that employees and their families can adapt smoothly to their new environments.

## Conclusion

Work-life balance in a global workforce is a multifaceted challenge that demands a combination of cultural sensitivity, time management, and flexible work arrangements. Achieving this balance is not only vital for employees' well-being but also crucial for the overall success of multinational companies. By addressing cultural differences, time zone challenges, and travel requirements, organizations can create an environment that supports work-life equilibrium.

Implementing flexible work arrangements and remote work policies further empowers employees to manage their work commitments in a way that aligns with their personal and family needs. Flextime, telecommuting, job sharing, and part-time options can all be tailored to the unique circumstances of a global workforce.

In the ever-evolving landscape of multinational companies, achieving work-life balance is an ongoing process that requires a commitment from both employers and employees. When individuals are empowered to balance their work and personal lives effectively, they become more engaged and productive, ultimately contributing to the success of the organization.

As multinational companies continue to expand and adapt to a globalized world, addressing work-life balance will remain a top priority. It is not merely a matter of policy but a shared responsibility that defines the way we work and live in the 21$^{st}$ century. Balancing the demands of a global workforce with personal and family life is a dynamic and evolving journey, and the key to success lies in understanding the diverse needs and aspirations of the people who make these multinational organizations thrive.

# Chapter 6. Career Development and Advancement Opportunities

## Introduction

Multinational companies (MNCs) have long been a beacon of career opportunities, offering a world of possibilities for individuals looking to grow and thrive in their professional lives. These organizations, often spanning multiple countries and industries, provide a unique platform for career development that is second to none. In this article, we will delve into the multifaceted landscape of career advancement within MNCs, exploring the various career paths available, the importance of employee growth and development programs, and ultimately, what it means to build a successful and fulfilling career in the world of multinational companies.

## Career Paths within MNCs

One of the defining features of MNCs is their sheer scale and complexity. These organizations operate across international borders, encompassing diverse functions, industries, and geographies. Within this expansive framework, career paths can take on a multitude of forms.

### 1. Functional Career Paths

Functional career paths in MNCs are the most common and well-defined. They involve progression within a specific department or role. Whether it's marketing, finance, human resources, or operations, MNCs offer employees the opportunity to start at entry-level positions and climb the ranks through various roles. Individuals can specialize in their chosen field, becoming experts and leaders in their respective areas.

For instance, in a multinational tech company, someone starting as a junior software developer can move up to become a senior software engineer, then a team lead, and eventually a department head, shaping the future of technology.

## 2. Cross-Functional Career Paths

Cross-functional career paths are another intriguing aspect of working in MNCs. These paths allow employees to explore different functions and departments, broadening their skill sets and knowledge. By transitioning from one area of the business to another, individuals gain a holistic perspective on the company's operations. This not only fosters adaptability but also encourages creativity and innovation.

Imagine a marketing specialist who, after a few years, takes on a role in the sales department. This move not only diversifies their skill set but also equips them with a more comprehensive view of the business, which can be invaluable for higher leadership positions.

## 3. Geographical Career Paths

In MNCs, geographical career paths open doors to explore various international offices and markets. These paths are perfect for those with a penchant for cultural immersion and a desire to understand global business dynamics. Employees who excel in such roles often become key players in the organization's expansion strategies.

A prime example would be a sales executive who starts in the domestic market and progresses to lead international sales efforts, requiring them to adapt to various cultures, regulations, and market nuances.

## 4. Leadership Career Paths

For ambitious individuals aiming for top leadership positions, MNCs offer specific leadership career paths. These paths include roles such as team leads, managers, directors, and even C-suite positions (executive or top-level management positions) like CEO (Chief Executive Officer), CFO (Chief Financial Officer), or CMO (Chief Marketing Officer). Advancement along these paths often requires not only technical competence but also strong leadership, strategic thinking, and the ability to navigate complex global landscapes.

A journey through leadership positions may begin with a project manager overseeing a small team and eventually lead to the role of a Chief Operating Officer (COO) responsible for global operations.

**Employee Growth and Development Programs**

MNCs understand that their success is intrinsically tied to the development of their employees. Consequently, they invest heavily in programs and initiatives that nurture talent, promote learning, and create opportunities for personal and professional growth.

## 1. Training and Development Programs

One of the cornerstones of career development in MNCs is the presence of comprehensive training and development programs. These programs cover a wide range of topics, from technical skills to leadership, communication, and cultural competence. Employees are often encouraged to take part in workshops, seminars, and online courses to acquire new skills and knowledge.

For example, a multinational pharmaceutical company may offer a structured training program to educate sales representatives about the latest drugs and treatment methods. This not only enhances their product knowledge but also keeps them at the forefront of industry advancements.

## 2. Mentoring and Coaching

Mentoring and coaching programs are a vital component of career development in MNCs. These programs pair employees with experienced mentors or coaches who guide them through their career journey. Mentors provide insights, advice, and a broader perspective, while coaches focus on specific skills and goals.

A junior marketing manager in an international advertising agency might be paired with a seasoned executive who can provide valuable advice on navigating the complexities of global advertising campaigns.

## 3. Leadership Development

Leadership development is of paramount importance within MNCs, and many organizations actively seek out potential leaders among their workforce. Leadership programs are designed to identify and groom individuals with the potential to assume critical leadership positions. These programs include leadership workshops, executive coaching, and opportunities for leadership roles in special projects.

A finance professional who exhibits exceptional strategic thinking may be selected for a leadership development program, which eventually paves the way for them to become the CFO.



One of the unique features of MNCs is the opportunity for international assignments. These can range from short-term projects to long-term postings in different countries. Such assignments not only expand employees' horizons but also contribute significantly to their personal and professional growth.

Consider an IT specialist who is selected for a six-month assignment in the company's Singapore office. This experience not only exposes them to a different work culture but also helps them build a global network and adapt to diverse working environments.

## Conclusion

In the realm of multinational companies, career development and advancement opportunities are as diverse as the companies themselves. The ability to explore various functional, cross-functional, geographical, and leadership career paths provides a rich and dynamic experience for professionals. Furthermore, the presence of robust employee growth and development programs equips employees with the skills, knowledge, and support necessary to excel in their careers.

In conclusion, a career in a multinational company is not just a job; it's a journey of personal and professional growth. It's an opportunity to be part of a global community, to understand different cultures, and to contribute to a company's success on a worldwide scale. For those willing to embrace the challenges and seize the opportunities, the world of multinational companies offers an exciting and rewarding path to a fulfilling career.

# Chapter 7. Compensation and Benefits in Multinational Companies

## Introduction

The global landscape of business has witnessed a significant transformation over the years, with multinational companies (MNCs) playing a pivotal role in shaping the way industries operate. These MNCs, with their expansive presence in multiple countries, have a diverse and dynamic workforce. One of the critical aspects that such companies need to carefully consider is the compensation and benefits they offer to their employees. In this article, we will delve into the intricate world of compensation and benefits in multinational companies, exploring the nuances of global compensation packages, international benefits, and incentives. By doing so, we aim to shed light on the strategies employed by MNCs to attract, retain, and motivate talent across borders.

## Analysis of Global Compensation Packages

### 1. The Complexity of Compensation in MNCs

Compensation in multinational companies is a multifaceted issue. It requires a keen understanding of local, national, and international labor markets, tax systems, and regulations. MNCs must carefully navigate the complexities of varying currencies, cost of living, and legal requirements in different countries. This calls for a compensation strategy that aligns the interests of the company with the expectations of its diverse workforce.

## 2. Equal Pay for Equal Work: The Challenge

One of the primary challenges faced by MNCs in managing compensation is ensuring equal pay for equal work. Disparities in wages across regions and countries can lead to dissatisfaction and inequality issues among employees. MNCs must take steps to address this, often by adopting global grading and job evaluation systems that can provide a benchmark for fair compensation.

## 3. Base Salary vs. Cost of Living Adjustments

While MNCs must offer competitive base salaries to attract top talent, they also need to consider cost of living adjustments. Employees working in higher-cost areas should receive additional compensation to maintain their standard of living. The challenge lies in determining an equitable method for calculating these adjustments across diverse geographies.

## 4. The Role of Currency Exchange Rates

Currency exchange rates can significantly impact the real value of compensation in multinational companies. MNCs often employ currency protection policies or mechanisms to shield employees from adverse fluctuations. However, these measures can be costly and complex to implement, requiring a thorough understanding of financial markets.

## 5. Expatriate Compensation

MNCs frequently deploy expatriates to work in different countries to facilitate knowledge transfer and skill development. Expatriate compensation packages are intricate, typically including base salary, housing allowances, education allowances, and sometimes hardship premiums. These packages need to be tailored to the unique circumstances of each expatriate assignment.

## 6. Bonuses and Incentives

In addition to base salary and cost of living adjustments, MNCs often employ bonuses and incentives to motivate their global workforce. These can include performance-based bonuses, profit-sharing plans, stock options, and long-term incentive plans. Aligning these incentives with the company's global goals and local performance can be a delicate balancing act.

## International Benefits and Incentives

## 1. Healthcare and Insurance

MNCs must address the varying healthcare systems and insurance requirements in different countries. Providing adequate health coverage is not only a legal obligation but also essential for employee well-being. Companies often partner with international insurance providers to create a comprehensive global benefits package.

## 2. Retirement Plans

Retirement plans are another critical component of international benefits. MNCs must ensure compliance with local pension schemes while providing globally competitive retirement options. Some companies opt for portable retirement plans that allow employees to carry their savings with them as they move across borders.

3. Leave Policies

Paid leave policies can differ significantly from one country to another. MNCs need to establish consistent leave policies that align with their values while respecting local regulations. Parental leave, vacation days, and public holidays all require careful consideration.

4. Relocation Assistance

When transferring employees across borders, MNCs often provide relocation assistance. This includes services such as visa processing, housing support, cultural assimilation programs, and language training. These services are essential for helping expatriates and their families adapt to their new surroundings.

5. Global Employee Assistance Programs

Multinational companies also offer Employee Assistance Programs (EAPs) on a global scale. EAPs provide support for employees dealing with personal or work-related challenges, including mental health issues, stress, and cultural adaptation. These programs help ensure employee well-being and productivity.

6. Cultural Sensitivity and Local Integration

Cultural sensitivity is a vital aspect of international benefits and incentives. MNCs should not only provide the necessary benefits but also promote cultural integration and sensitivity training to help employees adapt to new environments and interact effectively with local colleagues.

## Conclusion

Compensation and benefits in multinational companies are a multifaceted challenge. To compete effectively in the global market and attract top talent, MNCs must design compensation packages that are not only competitive but also equitable and adaptable to the unique demands of different regions and countries. An analysis of global compensation packages reveals the complexities of this task, from equal pay for equal work to managing currency exchange rates and expatriate compensation.

International benefits and incentives further illustrate the comprehensive nature of managing a global workforce. MNCs must provide healthcare and insurance, retirement plans, leave policies, and relocation assistance that not only comply with local regulations but also meet the expectations of their employees. The existence of global employee assistance programs and cultural sensitivity initiatives underscores the commitment of MNCs to the well-being and professional development of their global workforce.

In a rapidly evolving global business environment, MNCs are challenged not only to maintain a competitive edge but also to do so while respecting the diverse and ever-changing needs of their employees. The success of multinational companies in this regard ultimately depends on their ability to strike a delicate balance between a standardized global approach and the flexibility to adapt to local requirements. As these companies continue to expand their global footprints, compensation and benefits strategies will remain a critical factor in their overall success.

# Chapter 8. Gender Equality and Diversity in MNC Workforces

## Introduction

Multinational companies (MNCs) have become a vital force in the global economy, spanning various industries and regions. As these companies operate on a global scale, their workforces are often diverse, representing different cultures, backgrounds, and experiences. Promoting gender equality and diversity within MNC workforces is not just a matter of corporate responsibility, but it also makes good business sense. In this article, we will explore the significance of gender equality and diversity in MNCs and the steps they can take to create inclusive work environments.

## Promoting Gender Equality and Diversity at All Levels

Understanding the Business Case: The first step in fostering gender equality and diversity in MNC workforces is recognizing the compelling business case behind it. Diverse teams bring a wide range of perspectives, fostering innovation and creativity. Companies that embrace diversity tend to perform better, attract top talent, and are more appealing to a diverse customer base. By appreciating the value of diversity, MNCs can take the necessary steps to integrate it into their culture and practices.

Establishing Inclusive Policies: MNCs should develop and enforce clear policies that encourage gender equality and diversity. These policies may include anti-discrimination measures, equal pay for equal work, and support for work-life balance. Creating a workplace where every employee feels valued and respected is crucial for promoting diversity.

Education and Training: Companies should invest in training programs that address unconscious biases, cultural sensitivity, and inclusion. These programs can help employees and leadership teams become more aware of their biases and promote a more inclusive environment.

Recruitment and Talent Acquisition: A diverse workforce begins with diverse recruitment efforts. MNCs should actively seek candidates from various backgrounds and demographics, using inclusive language in job postings and leveraging diverse hiring panels to reduce bias.

Mentoring and Sponsorship Programs: Implementing mentoring and sponsorship programs can provide underrepresented employees with the support and opportunities needed to advance in their careers. Senior leaders can actively mentor and sponsor employees from different backgrounds, ensuring a more inclusive leadership pipeline.

**Leadership Roles for Women and Underrepresented Groups**

Leadership Development: MNCs should make leadership development programs accessible to everyone, regardless of their gender, race, or background. By providing equal opportunities for leadership development, organizations can ensure that talent rises through the ranks based on merit rather than demographics.

Diverse Leadership Teams: Encouraging diversity at the leadership level is critical for ensuring that decisions are made with a broad range of perspectives. MNCs should actively promote women and underrepresented groups to leadership positions, reflecting the diversity of their workforces.

Equal Pay and Opportunities: Achieving gender equality and diversity in leadership roles also involves addressing pay gaps. MNCs should regularly review their compensation practices to ensure that all employees are paid fairly for their roles, irrespective of their gender or background.

Transparent Career Paths: Companies should create transparent career paths and promotion criteria, ensuring that all employees understand the expectations and opportunities for advancement. This clarity helps to prevent bias and discrimination in career progression.

Employee Resource Groups: Establishing employee resource groups (ERGs) can provide a platform for underrepresented employees to network, share experiences, and advocate for change within the organization. These groups can serve as a valuable resource for both employees and leadership.

**Conclusion**

In a world characterized by increasing globalization, the importance of gender equality and diversity in MNC workforces cannot be overstated. Not only does diversity foster innovation and creativity, but it also aligns with the principles of social responsibility and fairness. MNCs must recognize the business case for diversity, and then actively work to promote it at all levels within the organization.

By establishing inclusive policies, offering education and training, implementing diverse recruitment efforts, and creating mentorship programs, MNCs can ensure that their workforces are representative of the world they operate in. Furthermore, the active promotion of women and underrepresented groups to leadership roles is essential for realizing the full potential of diversity within these organizations.

It is vital for MNCs to continuously evaluate and adapt their strategies for promoting gender equality and diversity. This includes addressing any unconscious biases and discrimination that may persist within the organization. It also involves promoting transparency and fairness in pay and career advancement opportunities.

In conclusion, gender equality and diversity are not just moral imperatives but also smart business strategies for multinational companies. As MNCs strive to create inclusive, diverse, and equitable workforces, they not only benefit their employees but also contribute to a more equitable and just global society.

# Chapter 9. Mentorship and Leadership Development Programs

## Introduction

Life in multinational companies is marked by a fast-paced, dynamic, and often demanding environment. In such organizations, the need for effective mentorship and leadership development programs cannot be overstated. These initiatives play a pivotal role in shaping the future of both the employees and the company itself. In this article, we will explore the significance of mentorship and leadership development programs in the context of multinational companies, shedding light on how they contribute to the career growth of employees and the cultivation of the next generation of global leaders.

## Mentoring and Coaching for Employees' Career Growth

### 1. Understanding Mentorship

Mentorship is a dynamic relationship between a seasoned, experienced professional (the mentor) and a less-experienced individual (the mentee). The primary aim of mentorship is to transfer knowledge, provide guidance, and offer support to the mentee, ultimately contributing to their professional development. Within the context of multinational companies, mentorship programs are essential for bridging knowledge gaps and fostering growth.

## 2. Mentorship as a Two-way Learning Process

Effective mentorship is a two-way learning process that benefits both the mentor and the mentee. Mentors gain fresh perspectives, innovative ideas, and a sense of fulfillment by contributing to the growth of their mentees. Meanwhile, mentees receive personalized guidance and access to the wisdom of those who have navigated the complex terrain of multinational corporations.

## 3. Building Stronger Employee-Employer Relationships

Mentorship programs enhance the bond between employees and their employers. These programs demonstrate the company's commitment to its employees' development and well-being. By fostering a culture of mutual respect and support, mentorship initiatives encourage employee loyalty and engagement.

## 4. Tailored Career Development Plans

Through mentorship, employees can create personalized career development plans. Mentors assist mentees in setting goals, providing feedback, and offering strategies to achieve career milestones. This tailored approach allows employees to map out their career trajectory within the company.

## 5. Knowledge Transfer

Multinational companies operate in diverse markets and cultural landscapes. Mentorship is a powerful mechanism for transferring not only knowledge about the company but also insights into different markets, consumer behaviors, and global business dynamics. This knowledge exchange is invaluable for employees who may need to adapt to different cultures and business environments.

**Developing the Next Generation of Global Leaders**

1. Leadership Development Programs

Leadership development programs in multinational companies serve as breeding grounds for future leaders. These programs are designed to identify and nurture high-potential individuals within the organization, equipping them with the skills and knowledge required to take on leadership roles. Such programs typically encompass a variety of developmental activities, including training, coaching, and experiential learning.

2. Identifying Leadership Potential

Recognizing leadership potential is the first step in developing future leaders. Multinational companies employ various assessment tools and strategies to identify employees who exhibit the qualities required for leadership positions. These may include exceptional problem-solving skills, emotional intelligence, adaptability, and a global mindset.

3. Structured Leadership Training

Leadership development programs provide structured training in areas such as decision-making, strategic thinking, team management, and cross-cultural communication. These programs are tailored to meet the specific needs and challenges that leaders in a multinational environment may encounter.

## 4. Mentoring as a Key Component

In many leadership development programs, mentorship plays a critical role. Senior leaders within the organization often serve as mentors to the emerging leaders. This mentorship ensures that the leadership skills being cultivated align with the company's values, culture, and strategic goals.

## 5. Experiential Learning and Cross-functional Exposure

Effective leadership development programs incorporate experiential learning opportunities, which expose participants to real-world leadership challenges. Moreover, participants are encouraged to work in cross-functional teams and engage in international assignments, giving them a broader perspective of the organization's global operations.

## 6. Global Mindset and Cultural Competence

Multinational companies require leaders with a global mindset and cultural competence. Leadership development programs emphasize the importance of understanding and respecting diverse cultural norms and business practices. By doing so, they prepare future leaders to effectively lead in cross-border contexts.

## 7. Succession Planning

Leadership development programs are an integral part of succession planning in multinational companies. These programs ensure that there is a steady pipeline of qualified individuals ready to step into leadership roles when needed, reducing the risk of leadership gaps that could disrupt business operations.

## Conclusion

In the ever-evolving landscape of multinational companies, mentorship and leadership development programs are indispensable tools for nurturing talent and driving organizational success. These programs are not isolated initiatives but rather integral components of a company's strategic approach to human capital development.

Mentorship programs provide employees with guidance, support, and a roadmap for career growth, fostering stronger bonds between employees and employers. They also facilitate knowledge transfer, helping employees adapt to the challenges of operating in diverse global markets.

Leadership development programs, on the other hand, serve as the cornerstone for identifying and cultivating the next generation of global leaders. By equipping high-potential individuals with the skills and experiences they need, these programs ensure that the company remains agile, innovative, and adaptable in the face of changing global business dynamics.

In the pursuit of grooming tomorrow's leaders, multinational companies should continually refine and expand their mentorship and leadership development programs. These initiatives not only benefit the individuals involved but also provide a competitive advantage for the organization as a whole, securing its future in the global marketplace. In this symbiotic relationship between employees and employers, mentorship and leadership development are the catalysts that drive personal and organizational growth, making life in multinational companies both fulfilling and prosperous.

# Chapter 10. Cross-Cultural Communication Challenges

## Introduction

In today's globalized world, multinational companies play a pivotal role in the international business landscape. These organizations, with their diverse workforce, have the unique challenge of fostering effective communication across cultures. Successful cross-cultural communication is not only essential for teamwork and productivity but also for building a harmonious work environment. This article delves into the complexities of cross-cultural communication challenges that individuals and multinational companies often encounter, exploring language barriers, communication issues, strategies for effective cross-cultural communication, and the importance of cultural sensitivity.

## Language Barriers and Communication Issues

One of the most obvious and persistent cross-cultural communication challenges in multinational companies is language barriers. These barriers can manifest in various ways, making it difficult for individuals from different linguistic backgrounds to communicate effectively.

Vocabulary and Language Proficiency: The most evident challenge arises when employees have varying levels of proficiency in a common language, such as English. Even when English is the chosen lingua franca, differences in vocabulary and accents can lead to misunderstandings. For example, a British English speaker might use different words or expressions than an American English speaker, causing confusion.

Idiomatic Expressions: Idioms, proverbs, and colloquialisms can be a source of miscommunication. An idiom in one culture may have no equivalent in another, leading to confusion or even unintentional humor. For instance, saying "killing two birds with one stone" in a cross-cultural meeting might be confusing to non-native English speakers.

Non-Verbal Communication: Non-verbal cues, such as gestures, facial expressions, and body language, can differ significantly across cultures. What might be a sign of agreement in one culture could indicate disagreement in another. For instance, a nod of the head can mean "yes" in some cultures and "no" in others.

Communication Styles: Different cultures have distinct communication styles. Some cultures are more direct and explicit in their communication, while others employ indirect and nuanced approaches. These variations can lead to misunderstandings, as an employee from a direct communication culture might perceive their colleague's indirect communication as evasive.

**Strategies for Effective Cross-Cultural Communication**

Navigating cross-cultural communication challenges is essential for multinational companies to thrive in the global marketplace. There are several strategies that organizations and individuals can employ to enhance their cross-cultural communication skills.

Language Training and Cultural Awareness: Providing language training and cultural awareness programs to employees can help bridge language and cultural gaps. These programs can offer insights into the nuances of a particular language, culture, and communication style.

Active Listening: Encouraging active listening is crucial in cross-cultural communication. Employees should focus on understanding the message being conveyed rather than formulating their response. This practice can prevent misunderstandings and foster more effective communication.

Feedback and Clarification: Encouraging employees to ask for feedback and clarification is vital. When in doubt, it is better to seek clarification than to make assumptions. This approach can prevent misunderstandings and lead to more productive interactions.

Cultural Sensitivity and Adaptation: Employees should be aware of cultural differences and adapt their communication style accordingly. This means being flexible and open to different ways of expressing ideas and opinions.

Use of Technology: Leveraging technology can aid cross-cultural communication. Video conferencing, instant messaging, and email can facilitate communication among geographically dispersed teams. However, it's important to be aware of potential technology-related challenges, such as time zone differences and technical issues.

Diverse Teams: Building diverse teams can help overcome some communication challenges. A diverse team often brings a variety of perspectives and experiences, which can lead to more creative problem-solving and an increased understanding of different cultures.

Conflict Resolution Skills: Cross-cultural communication can sometimes lead to conflicts. Providing employees with conflict resolution training can help address misunderstandings and maintain a harmonious work environment.

Patience and Empathy: Patience and empathy are critical when dealing with cross-cultural communication challenges. Employees should recognize that not everyone will share their cultural background or language skills. Being patient and empathetic can go a long way in building trust and rapport.

**Conclusion**

Cross-cultural communication challenges are an inevitable part of the modern workforce, especially in multinational companies. Language barriers, differences in communication styles, and cultural nuances can create hurdles, but with the right strategies, these challenges can be navigated effectively.

In a world where global collaboration is increasingly important, organizations must invest in programs that enhance language skills and cultural awareness among their employees. Promoting active listening, feedback-seeking, and adaptation to different communication styles can further foster effective cross-cultural communication.

Additionally, recognizing the value of diverse teams and investing in conflict resolution skills is essential for creating a positive work environment in multinational companies. Ultimately, patience and empathy are the cornerstones of successful cross-cultural communication, allowing individuals from diverse backgrounds to collaborate harmoniously and achieve shared goals.

By acknowledging and addressing cross-cultural communication challenges, multinational companies can leverage their diversity as a strength, leading to improved innovation, productivity, and a more inclusive work culture. In doing so, they pave the way for greater success in the global marketplace.

## Introduction

Life in multinational companies is often characterized by the excitement of working with diverse teams, the opportunity to travel and experience different cultures, and the potential for career growth. However, amidst the hustle and bustle of this corporate world, employee well-being and mental health often take a backseat. The fast-paced, high-pressure environment can lead to various challenges that affect the overall wellness of employees. In this article, we will explore the importance of employee well-being and mental health support in multinational companies, looking at various initiatives and strategies that can help employees thrive in this global workplace.

## Employee Wellness Programs and Initiatives

### 1. Health and Fitness Programs

One of the cornerstones of employee well-being is physical health. Multinational companies often provide access to fitness centers, gym memberships, and wellness activities. Encouraging employees to prioritize their physical health can lead to reduced absenteeism and improved productivity. These programs can also help foster a sense of community among coworkers as they engage in fitness challenges or group workouts.

## 2. Stress Management Workshops

Multinational companies often operate in high-stress environments due to global competition and tight deadlines. Providing stress management workshops and resources can equip employees with the tools to handle stress more effectively. Techniques such as mindfulness, meditation, and time management can significantly contribute to employees' well-being.

## 3. Flexible Work Arrangements

Flexibility in work arrangements, such as remote work options, flexible hours, or compressed workweeks, can be a game-changer for employees struggling to balance work and personal life. This adaptability helps employees manage their well-being, particularly in times of personal or family crises.

## 4. Nutrition and Diet Programs

Proper nutrition plays a vital role in employee well-being. Companies can provide educational resources, healthy snack options, and on-site cafeterias with nutritious choices. These initiatives promote healthier eating habits, leading to increased energy levels and overall health.

## 5. Mental Health Support

It is essential to recognize that well-being encompasses mental health. Multinational companies are increasingly focusing on mental health support. This includes providing access to confidential counseling services, Employee Assistance Programs (EAPs), and mental health awareness campaigns. Employees need a safe space to discuss their mental health concerns without fear of stigma.

## Addressing Mental Health Challenges in a Global Workforce

1. Cultural Sensitivity and Training

Multinational companies employ individuals from various cultural backgrounds, each with their unique perspectives on mental health. Cultural sensitivity training equips managers and colleagues with the knowledge and skills to provide support without unintentionally causing offense. It also fosters an inclusive and empathetic work environment.

2. Language Accessibility

Effective mental health support requires clear and open communication. In global workforces, language barriers can be a significant obstacle. Companies should ensure that mental health resources and services are available in multiple languages, making them accessible to all employees.

3. Managing Time Zone Differences

Global teams often work across different time zones, which can lead to irregular working hours and increased stress. Companies should implement strategies to manage time zone differences effectively. This might include staggered work hours, rotating meeting times, and encouraging time management techniques that align with an employee's specific time zone.

4. Crisis Response and Support

Multinational companies must have crisis response plans in place. This involves not only addressing individual employee crises but also responding to broader emergencies, such as natural disasters or political instability in various regions. Employees need to know that their employer is there to support them in times of crisis.

## 5. Remote Work and Isolation

The rise of remote work, accelerated by global events, has brought with it a unique set of mental health challenges. Employees may experience feelings of isolation and detachment from the company culture. Employers can help by fostering a sense of connection through virtual team-building activities, regular check-ins, and open communication channels.

## 6. Diversity and Inclusion

Mental health issues can affect individuals from all backgrounds. A commitment to diversity and inclusion not only promotes equality but also creates an environment where employees feel valued and supported. This inclusivity extends to mental health support, where all employees should receive the same level of care and assistance.

## Conclusion

In the dynamic world of multinational companies, prioritizing employee well-being and mental health support is not just a moral responsibility but a strategic advantage. A healthy and mentally resilient workforce is more productive, innovative, and better equipped to handle the challenges of a global workplace.

Employee wellness programs and initiatives are essential in promoting physical health and reducing stress. Stress management workshops, flexible work arrangements, and nutrition programs can empower employees to take control of their well-being.

Addressing mental health challenges in a global workforce is equally critical. Companies should invest in cultural sensitivity training, language accessibility, and crisis response plans to ensure that all employees, regardless of their background, receive the support they need. The isolation of remote work, time zone differences, and diversity and inclusion considerations all play a role in promoting mental health in a multinational context.

Ultimately, multinational companies that prioritize employee well-being and mental health support not only create a healthier and happier workforce but also foster a more productive and resilient global team. In the end, it's a win-win situation where both employees and the company benefit from these vital initiatives. To succeed in the global marketplace, investing in the well-being of your most valuable asset – your employees – is not just an option but a necessity.

## Introduction

Multinational companies (MNCs) operate in a dynamic and diverse global landscape, bringing together individuals from various cultural backgrounds, languages, and work experiences. These organizations face unique challenges when it comes to performance evaluation and feedback due to their multicultural nature. Effectively evaluating employee performance and providing constructive feedback is essential for driving organizational success, employee development, and team cohesion. In this article, we will explore the intricacies of performance appraisal systems in MNCs and the significance of feedback and goal-setting within a multicultural context.

## Performance Appraisal Systems in MNCs

Performance appraisal is a systematic process used by organizations to assess the job performance of their employees. In the context of multinational companies, performance appraisal systems play a pivotal role in aligning individual and team goals with the company's overall objectives. Here are some key aspects of performance appraisal systems in MNCs:

Cultural Sensitivity: Multinational companies employ individuals from diverse cultural backgrounds. An effective performance appraisal system must consider these cultural differences to ensure fairness and avoid biases. Cultural sensitivity training and guidelines can help evaluators understand the nuances of different cultures and how they influence work behaviors and expectations.

Objective Criteria: Establishing objective and measurable criteria for evaluating performance is crucial. MNCs often use key performance indicators (KPIs) or other quantifiable metrics that are consistent across all locations. These criteria help reduce subjectivity and promote transparency.

360-Degree Feedback: A 360-degree feedback approach involves gathering input from peers, subordinates, superiors, and other stakeholders to provide a comprehensive view of an employee's performance. In a multicultural context, this can be particularly valuable as it considers a broader range of perspectives and experiences.

Language Barriers: Language diversity is common in MNCs, and language barriers can impede effective communication during performance evaluations. To mitigate this, companies may invest in language training and translation services to ensure that feedback is clear and easily understood.

Global Performance Standards: Establishing uniform global performance standards is a challenge in MNCs due to variations in local market conditions and cultural expectations. Companies often strike a balance between global consistency and local adaptation by setting core standards while allowing some flexibility at the regional level.

**Feedback and Goal-Setting in a Multicultural Context**

Feedback and goal-setting are integral components of performance appraisal systems, and they play a crucial role in nurturing employee development and maintaining motivation. In the context of multinational companies, the process of providing feedback and setting goals becomes more complex due to the diversity of the workforce.

Cultural Communication Styles: Different cultures have varying communication styles, with some being more direct while others are more indirect. Understanding these nuances is essential for effective feedback. For example, a direct approach may work well with some employees, while others may prefer a softer, more indirect approach.

Feedback Frequency: MNCs often operate across multiple time zones and regions. This can impact the frequency and timing of feedback sessions. Some companies opt for real-time feedback using digital tools, while others implement regular scheduled reviews to accommodate different time zones.

Goal Alignment: Goal-setting should align with the organization's objectives and the individual's career aspirations. In a multicultural context, it is crucial to consider how cultural values and expectations may influence an employee's career goals. A one-size-fits-all approach may not be effective.

Cultural Diversity Training: MNCs can benefit from offering training programs that raise cultural awareness among employees and managers. These programs can help individuals understand the diverse backgrounds of their colleagues, reducing miscommunication and misunderstandings in feedback and goal-setting processes.

Feedback Delivery Skills: Managers in MNCs need to develop effective feedback delivery skills that are adaptable to different cultural contexts. Training and coaching can help them navigate conversations with sensitivity and respect for cultural differences.

Individualized Approaches: One of the challenges in MNCs is the need for individualized approaches to feedback and goal-setting. Managers should be prepared to tailor their strategies to each employee's unique cultural and professional background.

Cross-Cultural Team Dynamics: In a multicultural setting, team dynamics often involve diverse groups working together. Feedback and goal-setting should consider not only individual performance but also the impact on team cohesion and collaboration among employees from different cultural backgrounds.

## Conclusion

In the increasingly interconnected world of multinational companies, effective performance evaluation and feedback are vital for fostering employee growth, ensuring organizational success, and maintaining a harmonious work environment. Multinational companies need to acknowledge and address the unique challenges they face in these areas due to their diverse workforce. This includes adopting cultural sensitivity, setting objective criteria, employing 360-degree feedback, overcoming language barriers, and striking a balance between global and local performance standards in their performance appraisal systems.

Additionally, feedback and goal-setting must adapt to the multicultural context by considering cultural communication styles, feedback frequency, goal alignment, cultural diversity training, feedback delivery skills, individualized approaches, and cross-cultural team dynamics. Only by understanding and embracing the intricacies of diversity can multinational companies harness the full potential of their workforce.

In conclusion, performance evaluation and feedback are not only tools for measuring and improving individual performance but also instruments for fostering cultural understanding, collaboration, and innovation in multinational companies. Embracing diversity and cultural sensitivity in these processes can lead to stronger, more resilient organizations that thrive in an increasingly globalized world.

# Chapter 13. Employee Engagement and Retention Strategies

## Introduction

In today's globalized business landscape, multinational companies play a pivotal role in the world economy. These organizations operate across diverse cultures, time zones, and industries, employing a diverse workforce to achieve their global objectives. However, with the myriad opportunities and challenges that come with multinational operations, employee engagement and retention have become critical focal points for sustaining success. This article explores the significance of employee engagement and retention strategies within the context of multinational companies, shedding light on the methodologies and approaches to ensure a motivated, satisfied, and loyal global workforce.

## Measuring and Improving Employee Engagement

Employee engagement is the emotional commitment an employee has towards their organization. It goes beyond job satisfaction and touches upon their enthusiasm and dedication towards their role. For multinational companies, measuring and improving employee engagement can be particularly complex due to the diversity and geographic dispersion of their workforce. To address this, various strategies are employed:

1. Surveys and Feedback Mechanisms

To measure engagement, companies utilize surveys and feedback mechanisms. These tools provide valuable insights into employees' thoughts, emotions, and perceptions. Multinational corporations often administer these surveys in multiple languages to cater to their diverse workforce. Anonymous responses foster honesty and help companies assess the global employee sentiment accurately.

## 2. Cultural Sensitivity

Understanding and respecting cultural nuances is essential. Different regions have distinct work ethics, communication styles, and expectations. Multinational companies should tailor their engagement strategies to accommodate these variations. Employees must feel that their culture and values are recognized and respected.

## 3. Communication and Transparency

Effective communication is the backbone of engagement. Multinational corporations should establish transparent lines of communication and ensure that information reaches all employees promptly. This can involve using technology to bridge geographical gaps and creating a unified corporate culture.

## 4. Professional Development and Training

Providing opportunities for growth and development is a powerful engagement strategy. Multinational companies often facilitate cross-border training programs, mentoring, and career paths that cater to different regions. This not only boosts engagement but also helps with retention, as employees are more likely to stay with a company that invests in their professional development.

Recognizing and rewarding employees' efforts transcends geographical boundaries. Multinational corporations can employ global recognition programs, which may include monetary rewards, awards, or public acknowledgment. These initiatives promote a sense of belonging and motivate employees to remain engaged.

## Reducing Turnover in a Global Workforce

High employee turnover can be a significant concern for multinational companies, as it disrupts operations, incurs recruitment costs, and affects employee morale. Reducing turnover in a global workforce requires a multifaceted approach.

### 1. Tailored Onboarding Programs

Onboarding programs are structured processes that help integrate and orient new employees into an organization, ensuring a smooth transition and early engagement. A well-structured onboarding process that is adapted to the local culture and job requirements can make a significant difference in employee retention. Multinational companies should ensure that new hires feel integrated, informed, and valued from day one.

### 2. Flexible Work Arrangements

Flexibility in work arrangements, such as remote work options and flexible hours, can be a key retention strategy, especially in a global context. Different regions may have different expectations regarding work-life balance, and offering flexibility can help companies retain talent.

3. International Career Opportunities

Many multinational companies attract and retain talent by offering international career opportunities. These opportunities might include short-term assignments, cross-border transfers, or overseas postings. Such experiences can be highly motivating for employees and reduce turnover.

4. Mentoring and Coaching

Implementing mentoring and coaching programs can help employees adapt to the global environment. This support system can provide guidance, support, and a sense of belonging, particularly for expatriates or those working in foreign subsidiaries.

5. Competitive Compensation and Benefits

Offering competitive compensation packages and benefits is a universal retention strategy. However, it's crucial for multinational companies to ensure that these packages align with local standards and regulations, addressing any disparities or inequities.

6. Workplace Diversity and Inclusion

A diverse and inclusive workplace is attractive to talent, as it fosters a sense of belonging and equality. Multinational companies should actively promote diversity and inclusion and have policies and programs in place to support them.

7. Exit Interviews and Feedback

Understanding why employees leave is as crucial as retaining them. Exit interviews can provide valuable insights into areas where improvement is needed. Multinational companies should use this information to fine-tune their retention strategies continually.

## Conclusion

In the dynamic world of multinational companies, employee engagement and retention strategies are paramount to success. Engaged and satisfied employees are more productive, innovative, and loyal, which ultimately leads to higher profitability and growth. Reducing turnover in a global workforce not only minimizes recruitment costs but also fosters stability and knowledge retention.

To effectively engage and retain employees in multinational companies, it is essential to recognize the unique challenges posed by diverse workforces across multiple regions. Tailored approaches, cultural sensitivity, open communication, and investment in professional development are key components of these strategies. Moreover, reducing turnover demands a combination of well-structured onboarding programs, flexible work arrangements, international career opportunities, mentorship, competitive compensation, and a commitment to workplace diversity and inclusion.

In a globalized world, successful multinational companies understand that their most valuable assets are their people. By nurturing and empowering their workforce through effective engagement and retention strategies, these organizations are better equipped to thrive and contribute to the global marketplace while enriching the lives of their employees.

# Chapter 14. Global Employee Networks and Communities

## Introduction

In an increasingly interconnected and diverse world, multinational companies (MNCs) play a pivotal role in shaping the global landscape. These organizations transcend borders and cultures, bringing together individuals from various backgrounds and walks of life. Amidst this diverse tapestry, the importance of global employee networks and communities cannot be overstated. They serve as the connective tissue that binds the employees of multinational companies, offering support, fostering inclusivity, and promoting a sense of belonging. This article delves into the significance of global employee networks and communities in the context of life in multinational companies.

Multinational companies operate on a global scale, which means that their workforce often comprises people from different countries, cultures, and backgrounds. This diversity is a source of strength, bringing various perspectives and experiences to the table. However, it can also pose challenges in terms of integration, communication, and creating a sense of belonging among employees. Global employee networks and communities have emerged as a powerful solution to address these challenges and tap into the unique advantages of a diverse workforce.

## Building Connections and Support Systems for Employees

The first and most fundamental aspect of global employee networks and communities is their role in building connections among employees. These networks create opportunities for individuals to connect with their peers who share similar backgrounds, interests, or experiences. In a multinational company, it is not uncommon for employees to feel like a small fish in a big pond. By joining an employee network, individuals can find like-minded colleagues, fostering a sense of camaraderie and support.

Creating a Sense of Belonging: Employee networks provide a sense of belonging for employees who may be far from their home countries or working in unfamiliar environments. Whether it's an Asian employee network in a European office or a women's network supporting gender diversity, these groups enable individuals to connect with others who understand their unique challenges and experiences.

Mentorship and Guidance: Many global employee networks offer mentorship programs where more experienced employees guide newcomers. This not only helps employees integrate more smoothly into their roles but also ensures that they have a reliable source of advice and support.

Language and Cultural Assistance: Language barriers and cultural differences can create communication challenges in multinational companies. Employee networks often facilitate language exchange programs and cultural awareness initiatives, helping employees overcome these obstacles.

: An inclusive environment is one where all individuals, regardless of their background, identity, or abilities, are respected, valued, and provided with equal opportunities to participate and contribute. Employee networks promote an inclusive environment where employees are encouraged to bring their whole selves to work. This inclusivity, in turn, leads to higher job satisfaction, productivity, and retention rates.

## Employee Resource Groups and Affinity Networks

Employee resource groups (ERGs) and affinity networks are voluntary, employee-led organizations within a company that provide support, advocacy, and a sense of community for individuals who share common characteristics, backgrounds, or interests, fostering diversity and inclusion in the workplace. Employee resource groups (ERGs) and affinity networks are common structures within multinational companies to support employees. These groups typically revolve around shared characteristics or experiences, such as ethnicity, gender, sexual orientation, or disability, and aim to promote diversity, equity, and inclusion within the organization.

Ethnic and Cultural Networks: These networks bring together employees of a specific ethnicity or cultural background. For example, there may be a Hispanic network, an African-American network, or a South Asian network. These groups celebrate cultural heritage, raise awareness about cultural issues, and provide a platform for employees to connect with others who share their background.

Gender Diversity Networks: Gender diversity networks, such as women's networks, promote equality and support for employees regardless of gender. These groups often address issues related to gender inequality, mentorship for women in leadership roles, and the advancement of gender-diverse talent.

LGBTQ+ Networks: Affinity networks for LGBTQ+ employees and their allies help create an inclusive and accepting workplace for all. They work on fostering understanding, eliminating discrimination, and supporting employees who identify as LGBTQ+.

Disability and Neurodiversity Networks: These networks focus on creating a more accessible and inclusive work environment for individuals with disabilities or neurodiverse conditions. *Neurodiversity* is the concept that neurological differences, such as autism, ADHD (Attention Deficit Hyperactivity Disorder), and dyslexia, should be recognized and respected as natural variations in the human population, rather than as disorders, and that individuals with these differences have unique strengths and perspectives to offer. These networks advocate for reasonable accommodations, educate employees, and provide a platform for those with disabilities to connect and share their experiences.

Generational Networks: Some companies establish networks based on generational differences, such as millennials (born between the early 1980s and the mid-1990s to early 2000s) or baby boomers (born between 1946 and 1964). These networks promote intergenerational collaboration and understanding.

Interest-Based Networks: Beyond characteristics or backgrounds, some networks focus on shared interests or hobbies. These may include sports enthusiasts, book clubs, sustainability advocates, and more. These networks add an extra layer of diversity and inclusion by connecting employees based on their passions.

: In multicultural work environments, employees may find support and community in networks centered around their faith or religious beliefs. These networks promote understanding and respect among employees of different religious backgrounds.

## Conclusion

In the intricate tapestry of multinational companies, global employee networks and communities serve as a beacon of support, inclusivity, and connection. They play a pivotal role in building bridges among diverse employees, fostering a sense of belonging, and breaking down barriers that might otherwise impede communication and collaboration. By promoting the creation of these networks, MNCs not only harness the strengths of diversity but also demonstrate their commitment to equity and inclusion.

In a world that is becoming increasingly interconnected, MNCs have a unique opportunity to lead by example, not only in terms of their business practices but also in the way they nurture the well-being of their employees. Employee networks and affinity groups are emblematic of this commitment, reinforcing the idea that every employee's voice matters and is essential in creating a vibrant, inclusive, and successful multinational organization. They are a testament to the fact that, in the realm of multinational companies, the whole is greater than the sum of its parts when individuals from diverse backgrounds come together to support and learn from each other.

# Chapter 15. Conflict Resolution and Cultural Sensitivity Training

## Introduction

Multinational companies, with their diverse workforces and global operations, often find themselves navigating a complex landscape of cultural differences. These differences can be a source of strength, providing a wide range of perspectives and experiences, but they can also lead to conflicts that affect productivity, morale, and overall company performance. As such, one of the critical elements in maintaining harmony and fostering efficient operations in these diverse environments is conflict resolution and cultural sensitivity training. This article explores the significance of such training programs in multinational companies, delving into the strategies for managing conflicts arising from cultural differences, and highlighting the key components of effective training initiatives.

## Managing Conflicts Arising from Cultural Differences

Understanding Cultural Conflicts: The first step in effective conflict resolution is recognizing that cultural conflicts are an inevitable part of working in a diverse multinational company. These conflicts often stem from differences in communication styles, work ethics, values, and even non-verbal cues. Acknowledging the existence of these differences is crucial for addressing and managing conflicts effectively.

Open Communication: Open and honest communication is a cornerstone of conflict resolution in a multicultural environment. It's important to create a workplace culture where employees feel safe discussing cultural conflicts without fear of reprisal. Managers should encourage employees to voice their concerns and seek resolutions through constructive dialogue.

Cultural Competency: Developing cultural competency is essential for both employees and leaders. Understanding and respecting cultural nuances, such as hierarchies, communication norms, and decision-making processes, can help prevent misunderstandings and conflicts. This cultural awareness is a vital part of conflict prevention.

Mediation and Conflict Resolution Teams: Establishing dedicated mediation and conflict resolution teams can provide a structured and impartial approach to handling cultural conflicts. These teams should be composed of individuals with a deep understanding of different cultures and effective conflict resolution strategies. Their role is to mediate disputes, facilitate dialogue, and offer guidance on cultural sensitivity.

Conflict Analysis: Multinational companies should implement a systematic approach to conflict analysis. This involves identifying the root causes of conflicts, categorizing them based on cultural differences, and understanding how these conflicts impact the organization. With this information, companies can tailor their conflict resolution strategies to address specific cultural issues.

**Training Programs for Cultural Sensitivity**

Assessment of Training Needs: Before implementing cultural sensitivity training, companies should conduct a thorough assessment of their employees' needs. This assessment might include surveys, focus groups, or consultations with experts to identify the specific cultural challenges within the organization.

Customized Training Modules: It's crucial to develop training modules that are tailored to the company's specific cultural context. Generic one-size-fits-all training programs may not be as effective in addressing the unique cultural dynamics at play in multinational companies. Customization ensures that the content is relevant and relatable to the employees.

Interactive Workshops: Cultural sensitivity training should be engaging and interactive. Workshops, role-playing exercises, and case studies are effective ways to help employees understand different cultural perspectives and develop the skills necessary to navigate cultural differences.

Incorporating Real-Life Scenarios: Training programs should incorporate real-life scenarios and examples that employees might encounter in their day-to-day work. This helps bridge the gap between theory and practice, making the training more applicable and valuable.

Language Training: In multinational companies, language barriers can be a significant source of conflict. Offering language training, where relevant, can improve communication and reduce misunderstandings. This is especially important in regions where multiple languages are spoken within the company.

Leadership Training: Cultural sensitivity training isn't limited to employees; it should also be extended to leadership. Leaders set the tone for the organization, and their cultural awareness and sensitivity can significantly impact the company's culture. Leadership training can help executives lead by example in embracing cultural diversity and managing conflicts.

: Regular feedback and evaluation of cultural sensitivity training programs are essential to measure their effectiveness. Companies should use employee surveys, post-training assessments, and performance metrics to gauge the impact of the training and make necessary improvements.

## Conclusion

In the diverse and dynamic environment of multinational companies, managing conflicts arising from cultural differences is not a luxury but a necessity. Conflict resolution and cultural sensitivity training are pivotal in ensuring that these conflicts do not hinder productivity, teamwork, and overall company performance.

By acknowledging the inevitability of cultural conflicts and creating a culture of open communication, companies can proactively address issues as they arise. Understanding the cultural nuances that contribute to conflicts is essential, as is having dedicated mediation and conflict resolution teams to assist in finding solutions.

Cultural sensitivity training plays a critical role in preventing conflicts and equipping employees with the skills needed to navigate cultural differences successfully. Customized training modules, interactive workshops, and leadership training ensure that employees at all levels of the organization are culturally competent and capable of fostering an inclusive work environment.

Multinational companies that invest in these training programs not only create a harmonious workplace but also gain a competitive advantage in the global market. They attract top talent from diverse backgrounds, improve employee satisfaction, and ultimately enhance their ability to adapt to the ever-evolving landscape of global business.

In conclusion, for life in multinational companies to thrive, conflict resolution and cultural sensitivity training should be an integral part of their organizational culture. Recognizing the importance of cultural diversity and investing in the tools and strategies to manage conflicts arising from it are key steps in achieving success in the complex and rewarding world of multinational business.

## Introduction

The landscape of work is undergoing a profound transformation, driven by technology, globalization, and changing expectations. For employees of multinational companies, this transformation is particularly significant, as they navigate the complex and ever-evolving dynamics of the modern workplace. In this article, we will explore the future of work, examining the trends and challenges facing employees of multinational companies. From remote work and virtual teams to emerging trends in employee experience and engagement, we will delve into the forces shaping the way we work, interact, and thrive in a globalized world.

## Remote Work and Virtual Teams

Remote work has become a defining feature of the contemporary workforce. Accelerated by the COVID-19 pandemic, many multinational companies adopted remote work as a response to the crisis. However, it quickly became apparent that remote work was not merely a temporary solution; it was a glimpse into the future of work. Remote work is here to stay, and it comes with both opportunities and challenges for multinational company employees.

1. Opportunities of Remote Work

Remote work offers employees greater flexibility in managing their work-life balance. The ability to work from anywhere has opened up new possibilities for international assignments and cultural exchange, enhancing the diversity and inclusivity of multinational companies. It also reduces the need for commuting, which is beneficial for the environment and individual well-being.

2. Challenges of Remote Work

Despite its advantages, remote work poses unique challenges. Multinational company employees must contend with time zone differences, cultural variations in work expectations, and the potential for isolation and burnout. Building and maintaining strong relationships with colleagues can be more challenging when physical distance separates team members.

3. Virtual Teams

In a globalized workforce, virtual teams are increasingly common. These teams consist of members from diverse geographical locations who collaborate online. Managing virtual teams requires a unique set of skills, such as effective communication, cross-cultural understanding, and the ability to leverage technology to foster collaboration. For multinational company employees, being part of a virtual team can be both enriching and demanding.

**Emerging Trends in Employee Experience and Engagement**

As multinational companies adapt to the changing world of work, they are also reimagining the employee experience to attract, retain, and engage top talent. Here are some emerging trends in this domain:

## 1. Flexible Work Arrangements

The 9-to-5 workday is giving way to flexible work arrangements. Employees have increasing autonomy over their work hours, enabling them to align their work with their natural rhythms. Multinational companies are increasingly adopting flexible schedules and outcomes-based performance evaluations.

## 2. Wellness and Mental Health Support

Employee well-being is a priority for multinational companies. In recognition of the challenges posed by remote work and the need for work-life balance, companies are investing in wellness programs and mental health support. These initiatives include counseling services, mindfulness programs, and fitness resources.

## 3. Diversity, Equity, and Inclusion (DEI)

Multinational companies are making strides in promoting diversity, equity, and inclusion. They recognize the value of diverse perspectives and are actively working to create inclusive environments. This trend is not only a moral imperative but also a strategic advantage, as diverse teams are known to be more innovative and adaptable.

## 4. Hybrid Work Models

A hybrid work model combines in-person and remote work. This approach offers the best of both worlds, allowing employees to maintain a physical office presence while also benefiting from remote work opportunities.

Multinational companies are experimenting with hybrid models to balance the need for collaboration and flexibility.

## 5. Upskilling and Lifelong Learning

In a rapidly changing work environment, employees must continuously acquire new skills. Multinational companies are investing in upskilling and providing opportunities for lifelong learning. This not only benefits employees but also ensures that companies remain competitive in a dynamic global marketplace.

## 6. Technology and Automation

Automation and artificial intelligence are reshaping job roles. While some tasks become automated, new roles emerge, requiring different skills. Multinational company employees need to adapt to these changes, staying updated on the latest technological advancements and acquiring new digital skills.

## 7. Global Collaboration

Collaboration across borders is becoming the norm. Technology enables employees to work with colleagues from around the world, fostering cultural exchange and international business perspectives. However, this also necessitates the development of strong intercultural communication skills.

## 8. Data-Driven Decision-Making

Employee experience and engagement are increasingly informed by data analytics. Companies collect data on employee sentiment, engagement, and performance to make informed decisions about workplace policies and practices. This trend emphasizes the importance of transparency and trust in the employer-employee relationship.

## Conclusion

The future of work for employees of multinational companies is marked by both exciting opportunities and significant challenges. Remote work and virtual teams have revolutionized the way we collaborate and interact, offering flexibility and diversity but also requiring adaptability and strong communication skills.

Emerging trends in employee experience and engagement reflect a changing landscape in which companies prioritize well-being, diversity, and lifelong learning. These trends are crucial not only for attracting top talent but also for maintaining a competitive edge in a globalized world.

As we move forward, the ability to thrive in the future of work will depend on the willingness to embrace change, adapt to new technologies, and build cross-cultural competencies. Employees of multinational companies must be agile, resilient, and open to new possibilities as they navigate the complex and ever-evolving world of work. Ultimately, the future of work is about reimagining the way we work, connect, and live, and multinational companies and their employees are at the forefront of this transformative journey.

"Life in Multinational Companies" offers a comprehensive exploration of the dynamic world of global corporations and their diverse workforces. This insightful volume delves into the intricacies of working in multinational companies, spanning from understanding the concept of multinational companies and the rich tapestry of their workforces to addressing crucial topics such as cultural diversity, inclusivity, and global mobility.

With chapters dedicated to HR practices, work-life balance, career advancement, gender equality, mentorship, cross-cultural communication, and employee well-being, this book provides invaluable insights and practical strategies for both employees and employers in the complex multinational environment. It concludes by examining the future of work in the context of global corporations, shedding light on emerging trends and challenges that will shape the employee experience. "Life in Multinational Companies" is an indispensable resource for anyone navigating the dynamic world of global business and its intricate workforce mosaic.

# ABOUT THE AUTHOR

**Mr. C. P. Kumar** is a retired Scientist 'G' from National Institute of Hydrology, Roorkee, Uttarakhand, India. He is also a Reiki Healer and Chakra Balancing practitioner (with pendulum dowsing) and offers Emotional Freedom Technique (EFT) to help individuals with emotional issues. Mr. Kumar has authored many books on technical, spiritual, and social topics.

For further details, you may visit his webpage
https://www.angelfire.com/nh/cpkumar/virgo.html